GROUNDHOG DAY

Hannah Isbell

Enslow Publishing
101 W. 23rd Street
Suite 240
New York, NY 10011
USA

enslow.com

Published in 2017 by Enslow Publishing, LLC.
101 W. 23rd Street, Suite 240, New York, NY 10011

Library of Congress Cataloging-in-Publication Data

Names: Isbell, Hannah, author.
Title: Groundhog day / Hannah Isbell.
Description: New York, NY : Enslow Publishing, [2017] | Series: The story of our holidays | Includes bibliographical references and index.
Identifiers: LCCN 2016022182| ISBN 9780766083349 (library bound) | ISBN 9780766083325 (pbk.) | ISBN 9780766083332 (6-pack)
Subjects: LCSH: Groundhog Day—Juvenile literature.
Classification: LCC GT4995.G6 I73 2017 | DDC 394.261—dc23
LC record available at https://lccn.loc.gov/2016022182

Printed in China

To Our Readers: We have done our best to make sure all websites in this book were active and appropriate when we went to press. However, the author and the publisher have no control over and assume no liability for the material available on those websites or on any websites they may link to. Any comments or suggestions can be sent by e-mail to customerservice@enslow.com.

Photo Credits: Cover, p. 1 Brian E. Kushner/Moment Open/Getty Images; p. 4 Alex Wong/Getty Images; p. 6 Gregory K Scott/Science Source/Getty Images; p. 9 ElenaZet/Shutterstock.com; p. 11 Martin Lehmann/Shutterstock.com; p. 12 Erik Mandre/Shutterstock.com; p. 14 Grisha Bruev/Shutterstock.com; p. 16 Archie Carpenter/Getty Images; p. 18 Education Images/Universal Images Group/Getty Images; p. 20 Jeff Swensen/Getty Images; P. 21 © Ron S Buskirk/Alamy Stock Photo; p. 22 Andrew Burton/Getty Images; p. 25 The Boston Globe/Getty Images; p. 27 Brent Hofacker/Shutterstock.com; p. 29 photo by Karen Huang.

Contents

Punxsutawney Phil sits on the shoulder of his handler during a Groundhog Day celebration at Gobbler's Knob.

Chapter 1

An Unusual Morning

Early in the morning on February 2nd, thousands of people gather in towns and cities across the Northeast of the United States to watch and wait. What are they waiting for? They are waiting to see whether a big rodent called a groundhog will see its shadow. This is Groundhog Day!

The largest Groundhog Day celebration is in Punxsutawney, Pennsylvania. As many as 30,000 people make their way to Gobbler's Knob to see Punxsutawney Phil, the most famous groundhog in the United States. Men in suits and top hats carry him out on stage as the crowd looks on. The folklore tells that if it is cloudy that day and he does not see his shadow, then spring will come early that year. But if the sun is shining and there's a shadow to see, there will be six more weeks of winter.

The People of Punxsutawney have a special home for Phil. Groundhogs are also called woodchucks or marmots. They live underground in burrows, and hibernate in the winter.

In different towns, other groundhogs are celebrated as they look for their shadows. After the groundhogs make their predictions, the news is reported across the country. The people who gathered to watch groundhogs in different towns stay to enjoy festivities with plays, music, food, and fun!

It may sound a little strange, or even a little silly. After all, can a groundhog really predict the weather? However, the traditions of Groundhog Day are very, very old.

Chapter 2

Groundhog Who's Who

Groundhogs can be found across much of North America, and go by many names, including woodchucks, whistlepigs, and thickwood badger.

Groundhogs like to live by themselves and in open country, like fields and meadows, or on the very edges of woods. They sometimes skirmish, or fight, over territory, but mostly will hide in their burrows if they feel threatened. If their burrow or offspring are in danger, though, groundhogs will fight viciously to protect them, using their large front teeth and claws.

They have two coats of fur to keep them warm, a dark grey undercoat, and a coat of longer hairs on top. While may be small, they have very strong limbs, equipped with thick curved claws. This makes them powerful diggers. They dig deep burrows, and never stray too far from their dens. It is there that they hibernate during the winter, only emerging when the weather starts to warm up in the spring.

This groundhog has just come out of its burrow. Groundhogs eat mainly plants, but they will eat bugs and other small animals, too.

Chapter 3

Ancient Roots

In America, Groundhog Day was first adopted as a holiday in 1887, but the traditions date back much, much further than that. The holiday has ancient roots.

Ancient Pagan Beliefs

Some ancient myths tell of badgers and bears predicting the weather. Ancient Germanic beliefs were closely tied to nature. The changing of the seasons, called equinoxes, were very important to the pagans of Northern Europe. Animals were important in ancient religions, too.

Badgers and bears hibernate during the winter and come out of their burrows and dens in the spring. Because of this,

A groundhog is a large rodent, about the size of a cat. They can be 16 to 26 inches (40.6–66 centimeters) long and usually weigh between 4 and 9 pounds (2–8 kilograms).

One ancient myth tells that if a bear comes out of its den and into the sun, it will be scared by its shadow and run back inside. It will then hibernate longer and keep spring from coming until it wakes up.

people saw the animals' behavior as signs of the vernal equinox, the beginning of the spring season. If the weather was mild, the animals would stay outside, but if the weather was bad, they'd go back into their dens.

These myths are many thousands of years old. They are part of the origins of Groundhog Day.

To celebrate badgers and bears coming out of hibernation, people would dress in bear costumes and have festivals. They lit bonfires as symbols of the return of sunlight in spring.

Imbolc

The return of sunlight in spring was important to the ancient Celts too. They celebrated the coming of spring on February 1st. This holiday was called Imbolc. The ancient Celts believed in many gods and goddesses. On Imbolc, they lit candles, built fires in their hearths, and carried bright torches for the goddess Brigid.

The holiday of Imbolc is so ancient that it dates back to prehistory. Today, Christians and Catholics honor Brigid as Saint Brigit. Candles are lit for her on the day the Celts celebrated Imbolc.

Candles are lit in a church for Candlemas.

Candlemas

For Christians, February 2nd is a very old holiday called Candlemas. Candlemas has been celebrated for about 1,600 years. It is also a celebration of light. During Candlemas, all candles in churches are lit.

Chapter 4

The Blending of Traditions

Over more than a thousand years, the traditions and beliefs from different peoples blended together. Pagan, Celtic, and Christian customs were shared among the peoples of Europe. They began to look to the weather on Candlemas Day as a sign: a cloudy Candlemas Day meant spring would come, and a sunny day meant a long winter. This tradition was most common in Germany.

Coming to America

When Europeans colonized America, many German immigrants settled in the eastern United States. They brought

The people in Punxsutawney dress formally as a nod to the old traditions in which Groundhog Day has its roots.

their traditions and beliefs with them. There was even an old German poem that linked Candlemas Day to the changing seasons:

> For as the sun shines on Candlemas Day,
> So far will the snow swirl until May,
> For as the snow blows on Candlemas Day,
> So far will the sun shine before May.

The ancient tales of bears and badgers predicting the changing seasons came with the settlers. So did the tradition of checking the weather on Candlemas Day to see if spring would come early or if winter would linger. These traditions all came together into what is now Groundhog Day.

European immigrants settling in North America brought their culture with them, including religion, customs, and traditions.

Chapter 5

An American Holiday

Groundhog Day began as a Pennsylvania German custom, but today it is a popular holiday all over the United States. Groundhogs are native to North America. They replaced badgers and bears in the immigrants' folklore, and while the ancient tales began in Europe, only in America will you find groundhogs predicting the weather!

In many cities and towns, the mayor hosts the celebrations as the local groundhog makes its prediction. However, the biggest celebrations can still be found in Pennsylvania, especially in communities with strong German ancestry.

Today, people may dress up as groundhogs to celebrate the day.

In New Orleans, a coypu, also known as a nutria, looks for its shadow!

Fersommlinge

In Southeastern Pennsylvania, Groundhog Lodges hold special celebrations on Groundhog Day called *fersommlinge*. In addition to the usual tradition of watching the groundhog in the morning,

In Staten Island, New Yorkers watch Staten Island Chuck look for his shadow

there are speeches, skits, and food. People are only allowed to speak Pennsylvania German at the festival. If they speak English they have to pay a penalty! Usually it's just a nickel, dime, or quarter, though!

Even in the United States, Groundhog Day customs vary from place to place. In Alaska, Groundhog Day is called "Marmot Day." But in some states, it's more than just the name that changes! In Red Rock Canyon, Nevada, a desert tortoise named Mojave Max makes the yearly weather prediction. In Louisiana coypus take the important role in the state's own "Cajun Groundhog Day." On February 1st, Claude the Cajun Crawfish, from Shreveport, predicts the weather for the upcoming Mardi Gras season!

Chapter 6

So, Does It Work?

Can a groundhog really predict whether spring will come early? Meteorologists are scientists who study the weather. Climate scientists study weather patterns over hundreds, thousands, and millions of years. They all agree that groundhogs aren't very good at telling when spring will come.

A team of researchers in Canada looked at all the predictions of groundhogs in 13 cities for the past 40 years. They compared those to the recorded weather for those years. They found that the groundhogs were right less than half the time! The

If you want a real prediction for when spring will arrive, it is probably better to listen to a meteorologist. But it's not as much fun as watching the groundhog look for its shadow!

National Climatic Data Center said, "The groundhog has no talent for predicting the arrival of spring, especially in recent years."

The truth is that Groundhog Day is not a very good way to know what the upcoming weather will be. Whether a groundhog sees its shadow or not on February 2 can't really tell us if spring will come early. It doesn't tell us if the winter will be a long one. However, Groundhog Day is still an important part of American culture. It is a special holiday. It is unique to America, blending customs and beliefs from all over the world. Above all, it is a time to brighten up the coldest part of the year with a bit of fun!

Cooking on Groundhog Day

With its German roots, what better snack to make to celebrate Groundhog Day than German apple brown bread? Let's get cooking!

German Apple Brown Bread Ingredients:

2 medium tart apples
1/4 cup unsalted butter
1/3 cup light or dark molasses
1/3 cup honey
1 cup rye flour
1 cup whole-wheat flour
1 cup cornmeal
2 teaspoons baking soda
1 teaspoon salt
2 cups low-fat buttermilk

Directions:

1. Have an adult help you peel, core and chop the apples.
2. In large bowl, beat butter until softened. Blend in molasses and honey.
3. In another bowl, combine the rye and wheat flours, cornmeal, baking soda, and salt.
4. Slowly add half of the flour mixture to the butter mixture, blending just until moistened. Then blend in half of the buttermilk and the rest of the flour mixture.
5. Add the remaining buttermilk and mix until ingredients are blended.
6. Stir in apples.
7. Spoon into two lightly greased 9-by-5-inch bread pans and have an adult help you bake at 325°F for one hour or until a toothpick inserted into the centers comes out clean. Cool in pans 10 minutes before removing. Serve warm or cooled.

* Adult supervision required.

Groundhog Day Craft

Groundhogs are native to North America. They prefer to live in open areas like meadows and fields, or on the edges of the woods. They never stray far from their burrows.

You can create a Groundhog Day shadow box to show a groundhog in its habitat. Take it outside early in the morning or put it in a window to see if your groundhog casts a shadow!

Here are the supplies you will need:

a shoebox
scissors
heavy brown construction paper
twigs and small rocks
small white cotton balls
1 or 2 pipe cleaners
glue
crayons, colored pencils, or markers

Directions:

1. Turn the shoebox on its side horizontally and cut off the top.

2. Color the background of your groundhog's habitat. Remember, the groundhog likes open spaces or the edges of forests. You might draw the sky, trees, bushes, grass, and flowers.

3. Glue white cotton balls to the sky for clouds. You can pull the cotton balls apart to make the clouds any shape you like!

4. Color the ground of the habitat. Remember to include your groundhog's burrow!

5. Glue small rocks and twigs to the ground of your groundhog's habitat.

Groundhog Shadow Box

6. To make your groundhog, draw a groundhog on brown construction paper. Make sure it is nice and big, about the size of your fist. You can use pictures from the book to help you draw.

7. Cut out your groundhog.

8. Glue a pipe cleaner to the back of your groundhog. Leave half of the pipe cleaner sticking out from the bottom like you were making a puppet.

9. When the glue is dry, glue the other half of the pipe cleaner to the ground of your shadowbox. Bend the pipe cleaner to stand your groundhog up. If your groundhog is heavy, it might need two pipe cleaners to hold it!

*Safety Note: Be sure to ask for help from an adult, if needed, to complete this project.

Glossary

ancient Belonging to a very distant past; very old or long ago.

Candlemas A Christian festival held on February 2nd where candles are blessed.

folklore The traditional beliefs, customs, stories, and songs of a culture or community that are passed from one generation to the next by word of mouth.

hibernate To spend the winter in a dormant, or sleep-like, state.

immigrants People who move from one country to live permanently in another one.

meteorologist One who studies weather and climate patterns and makes predictions about the weather.

pagan One who follows a religion with many gods rather than one God.

prediction A guess about something that could happen in the future.

tradition A set of customs or beliefs that have been passed from generation to generation.

vernal equinox The day in spring where night and day are almost equal in length. This occurs around March 20 in the northern parts of the world and September 22 in the southern parts.

Learn More

Books

Meister, Carrie. *Groundhogs*. Minneapolis, MN: Jump! 2015.

Murray, Julie. *Groundhog Day*. Pinehurst, NC: Buddy Books, 2014.

Pearlman, Robb. *Groundhog's Day Off*. New York, NY: Bloomsbury USA, 2015.

Websites

National Geographic Kids: Groundhog
kids.nationalgeographic.com/animals/groundhog/#groundhog-with-babies.jpg
   Learn about groundhogs in the wild.

NOAA National Centers for Environmental Information: Groundhog Day
www.ncdc.noaa.gov/customer-support/education-resources/groundhog-day
   Information on Groundhog Day as well as a chart on whether the groundhog saw his shadow in a given year.

The Punxsutawney Groundhog Club
www.groundhog.org
   Learn about the history of Groundhog Day, some fun facts, and all the news you need to know about Punxsutawney Phil.

Index